CRANKS

SALADS & DRESSINGS

Compiled by Daphne Swann

Cranks is indebted to Jane Suthering, the well-known home economist. She has worked with Cranks on all their recipe books and has adapted, devised and tested the recipes in this latest series.

Pottery for photography kindly loaned by Craftsmen Potters Shop, Marshall Street, London W.1.

As a rough guide, all the recipes serve 4–6 people. This of course very much depends on individual appetites and on the occasion for which the salads are used.

© Text Cranks Ltd 1988
© The Work Guinness Publishing Ltd 1988
Editor Beatrice Frei
Art editor David Roberts
Illustrations Suzanne Alexander, Edward Bawden and Jane Lydbury
Cover Ashley Lloyd
Photographs Grant Symon

Published in Great Britain by Guinness Publishing Ltd,
33 London Road, Enfield, Middlesex, England.

Cranks salads & dressings.
1. Salads
I. Cranks Limited
641.8'3   TX807

ISBN 0-85112-871-8

Typeset by Ace Filmsetting Ltd, Frome, Somerset
Printed and bound in Spain by Graficas Reunidas S.A., Madrid

INTRODUCTION

When Cranks opened its first restaurant 27 years ago (in Carnaby Street in London's Soho) its name exactly reflected how most people viewed wholefood and vegetarian restaurants – nutty in more senses than one! Now, of course, the lonely furrow that Cranks then ploughed has become the broad highway for a great many.

From the very beginning Cranks became something of a cult and throughout has remained the benchmark by which all other similar enterprises have to be judged. Not only has there been an unswerving commitment to wholefood and vegetarian food without additives or preservatives (to this day Cranks still uses flour from Pimhill Farm in Shropshire, which was one of the first to become totally organic) but there has also been a vigorous experimentation, innovation and creation of new dishes. And although now the food served at any of Cranks expanding family of restaurants is sophisticated by comparison with the relatively simple fare of the earliest days, there still remains a satisfying practicality and unfussiness in the recipes which is a refreshing change from the pretentiousness of many restaurants and cookbooks.

The continual creation of new dishes has, over the years, produced a vast number of tried and tested recipes – and it's from this repertoire of new dishes that the very best have been selected for inclusion in this series of books.

NOTES ON INGREDIENTS

*B*utter Cranks recommends using an unsalted butter. Vegetarian margarine may, of course, be substituted in all recipes where butter is stated.

Cheese A wide variety of vegetable rennet cheeses is now being produced. At present there are at least 50 varieties – most health food stores and some supermarkets will offer a good choice. For further information, contact The London Cheese Company, Unit 9, Cedar Way, Camley Street, London NW1.

Coconut Can be bought in various forms – desiccated or shredded (which is finely grated and dried) or creamed. This is sold in bars or tubs and can be broken off and melted for use in cooking. Coconut milk powder is sold like dried milk. All can be found in good health food shops or oriental shops.

Eggs Cranks only uses free-range eggs in its bakeries and therefore recommends them in all recipes. Be sure to look on the label for the words "free range" when purchasing.

Kidney beans These must be fast boiled for a minimum of 15 minutes to destroy a poisonous substance they contain. They should never be sprouted raw as they are toxic until thoroughly cooked.

Nuts When using nuts in salads it is preferable to toast them beforehand to bring out the flavour. Place nuts on a baking sheet in the oven at 350°F/180°C/gas mark 4 for 10–15 minutes or until golden. Alternatively, place under a pre-heated grill and turn regularly until golden.

Oil Sunflower, safflower and soya oils are all good to use for salads and cooking, being mild in flavour and low in saturated fats. However, olive oil gives a particularly good flavour for certain dressings.

Soya sauce A dark salty sauce made from fermented soya beans and used here to add a distinctive flavour to dressings.

Sprouting Most beans, pulses and grains are very easy to sprout at home. Soak a small handful of beans overnight, then drain and rinse well. Place in a large jar, covered securely with a piece of muslin and leave in a dark warm place. Rinse well morning and night and drain off excess water. Continue the process for two or three days until sprouts are at least half an inch (1.5 cm) long. Wash well before eating. Many commercially-sprouted beans are also available in food shops. Kidney beans must never be used for sprouting.

Sugar Unrefined brown sugar is used in some of the dressings to sweeten them slightly. It may be omitted or replaced by honey.

Tofu A soya bean curd with a soft delicate texture and pale in colour. Sold in slabs or slices, available plain (silken or firm), with herbs, smoked or marinated. Keep refrigerated.

Wheat Wholewheat berries are the nutritious whole grain of wheat with none of the germ or outer layers removed. They are delicious when cooked in salads or savoury dishes. Bulghar wheat is a preparation of cracked wheat which simply requires soaking before eating. Rich in the B vitamins, phosphorus and iron.

Yoghourt Natural yoghourt is a good form of protein, low in fat if made with skimmed milk, and a good source of calcium. Ideal for dressings.

TO TOSS A SALAD

A tossed salad should be one in which the ingredients are just coated with dressing so that they glisten. There should not be an excess of dressing in the bottom of the salad bowl. To do this, place the salad in a large bowl, pour a little dressing over the salad, and using salad servers or two spoons, carefully turn the salad ingredients in a rotating movement until evenly coated. Add a little more dressing if necessary and repeat.

As a general rule, green leaf salads should be tossed just before serving. Root vegetable salads, marinated salads and those tossed in mayonnaise will improve if dressed the day before, and will keep in a refrigerator for two or three days. The exceptions to this include watery vegetables, particularly tomatoes, which lose their flavour if kept for more than 24 hours.

UNUSUAL VEGETABLES

With notes on Fruit, Flowers and Herbs

A lot of the goodness in fruit and vegetables lies in, or just below, the skin so wash, wipe, scrub and trim them as necessary, but never peel unless absolutely essential!

Aubergine Dark purple, white or purple mottled pear-shaped vegetables which can be bitter when cooked. To prevent this, slice or dice and sprinkle with salt. Leave for 30 minutes to extract the bitter juices. Rinse well and dry thoroughly.

Beetroot Scrub well, if necessary discard any rough skin. Top and tail and coarsely grate if eating raw. To cook, leave whole and steam or cook in boiling water for up to 1 hour depending on size, until tender. Cool and rub off the skin.

Celeriac A large round knobbly root closely related to celery with a similar flavour. It may be eaten raw or cooked.

Citrus fruits Thoroughly wash all citrus fruit rinds before using, to remove any chemical deposits – better still, use organically-grown fruit.

Fennel Often known as *Florence fennel*, it is a large bulbous root, pale green in colour with stalks and herb fronds at the top. It has a delicate flavour similar to aniseed and may be eaten raw or cooked.

Flowers A selection of edible flower heads is now available from speciality food shops and some supermarkets. You can, of course, also pick your own from the garden or countryside. These include *nasturtiums, marigolds, carnations, borage, pansies, clover* and *roses*, as well as the flower heads from herbs such as *thyme, basil* or *sage.*

Herbs It is always preferable to use fresh herbs in salads and these are more and more commercially available as well as straight from the garden. Occasionally, dried herbs may be substituted in dressing recipes, in which case use 1 tsp (5 ml) in place of 1 tbsp (15 ml) fresh, chopped herbs.

Jerusalem artichokes Small knobbly tubers with a distinctive sweet, nutty flavour, best eaten cooked.

Mangetout These sweet crisp flat peapods have tiny "undeveloped" peas inside. Translated, the word means "eat all", but they should be topped and tailed, and older pods may need stringing. May be used raw, but their colour is heightened by blanching.

Mushrooms A variety of cultivated mushrooms is available which includes the *Shiitake, Oyster* and *Chestnut* as well as the common mushroom in button, flat or cup shapes. Wild mushrooms such as *Chanterelles, Ceps, Girolles* and *Morels* are appearing in the shops, but do still tend to be quite expensive. All mushrooms should be wiped only and their stalks scraped clean with a small sharp knife. Cultivated mushrooms can all be eaten raw, but it is perhaps a good precaution to sauté wild mushrooms before eating them.

Okra Five- or six-sided green pointed pods with large white seeds sometimes known as *Ladies fingers*. Best eaten cooked and preferably sautéd as blanching or stewing tends to make them very glutinous.

Salad leaves

Batavia A large crisp lettuce made up of light green leaves with slightly frilly edges.

Chicory Spear-shaped white heads made up of individual leaves with yellowish tips, slightly bitter in flavour, but this can be reduced by removing a small triangular shape from the core with a sharp knife.

Chinese leaves Pale green elongated leaves with long fleshy white stalks densely packed together to form large heads.

Escarole Broad green leaves surrounding a yellow heart. The leaves have a slightly bitter tang.

Frisee Sometimes known as *Curly endive*, has frilly wispy green leaves becoming yellow towards the heart. It also has a slightly bitter flavour.

Iceberg An American variety of lettuce with tightly packed, very crisp leaves forming a large round head. Keeps exceptionally well.

Lamb's Also known as *Corn salad* or *Mache*, it has small velvety green leaves with a delicate, slightly bitter flavour.

Little gems A compact variety of dwarf cos lettuce which may be served whole.

Lollo rosso Frilled green leaves tinged with red make up this very attractive lettuce.

Oak leaf Also known as *Feuille de chene*, this is a loose-leafed heartless lettuce with jagged deep bronze leaves.

Quattro stagioni An Italian round lettuce with glossy crinkly leaves heavily tinged with a red-bronze colour.

Radicchio Sometimes known as *Red chicory*, it has crinkled dark red leaves with broad white veins forming small round heads. Radicchio has a slightly bitter flavour.

Sweetcorn Available as the traditional cobs, which should have their leaves and silken threads removed before cooking in boiling water with a spoonful of sugar, and never salt, added.

Baby or *Miniature* corn cobs are now readily available and these are about 3 inches (7.5 cm) long. They can be eaten raw or cooked.

SALADS & DRESSINGS

One of the most exciting things about salads, apart from eating them is the making of them – there are so many possibilities with the enormous variety of fruits and vegetables now available and the fun of experimenting with different flavours, textures and colours is endless.

In this book we have introduced some unusual combinations like warm wheatberry salad – a meal in itself – or the delicately flavoured melon and almond salad – also a variety of salads using fresh fruits, nuts, edible flower heads, fresh herbs and introducing some of the more unusual salad leaves now on the market. In addition, there are some cooked vegetable salads, marinated salads, salads using proteins like cheese, eggs, beans and pulses, pastas and rice.

There is an explanatory section on unusual fruits and vegetables. When buying ingredients for salads, try and get organically-grown and unsprayed fruit and vegetables – these are now more readily available, and the more demand there is for them, the more supply we'll get!

Choosing the right dressing plays a vital part in the success of a salad. The flavour of it should complement and highlight the salad ingredients, adding piquancy to the taste – we have indicated which dressing would go well with each salad but there is no reason why one cannot mix and match according to personal taste. Dressings store well in a refrigerator and it is a good idea to keep about a pint of the basic French dressing and mayonnaise always at the ready! Notes on ingredients can be found on page 4–6 with a section on how to toss a salad.

SPICY POTATO SALAD
in a curry dressing

A straightforward everyday salad with a touch of spice!

Potatoes 1 lb (450 g)
Curry dressing (see p. 80) ¼ pt (150 ml)
Medium carrots 2
Celery sticks 4
Salt & pepper to taste

Cut the potatoes into large dice and steam or boil for about 10 minutes, or until tender. Drain and mix with the curry dressing.

Leave to go cold.

Thinly slice the carrots and celery and add to the potatoes. Toss well and season to taste.

12

BULGHAR WHEAT SALAD
with fresh basil

Rich in the B vitamins, phosphorus and iron, bulghar
wheat is an ideal base for a salad.

Bulghar wheat 4 oz (100 g)
Tomatoes 8 oz (225 g)
Cucumber 4 oz (100 g)
Onion 1 oz (25 g)
Olive oil 4 tbsp (60 ml)
Lemon juice 1 tbsp (15 ml)
Fresh basil, thinly sliced 2 tbsp (30 ml)
Salt & pepper to taste

Wash the bulghar wheat, then just cover with boiling
water and leave to soak for 30 minutes. Drain well and
squeeze out excess water. Finely chop the tomatoes,
cucumber and onion. Mix the olive oil, lemon juice,
fresh basil and salt & pepper together. Place all the
ingredients in a bowl and mix well.

CARROT & CARAWAY
MAYONNAISE

A favourite in the early days of Cranks – this salad
is quick, simple and delicious!

Carrots 1 lb (450 g)
Currants 2 oz (50 g)
Caraway seeds 2 tsp (10 ml)
Mayonnaise (see p. 83) ¼ pt (150 ml)
Salt & pepper to taste

Finely grate the carrots, then mix well with the
remaining ingredients.

NUT & RICE SALAD
in a turmeric dressing

Long grain brown rice 8 oz (225 g)
French dressing (see p. 79) ¼ pt (150 ml)
Turmeric 1 tsp (5 ml)
Watercress 4 oz (100 g)
Hazelnuts, toasted 2 oz (50 g)
Desiccated coconut 2 oz (50 g)
Salt & pepper to taste

Cook the rice in boiling water for 30–35 minutes until
just tender. Drain well. Mix the French dressing with
the turmeric and add to the rice. Leave to go cold.

Chop the watercress and hazelnuts and add to the
rice with the coconut. Mix well, and season to taste.

DRUNKEN POTATO SALAD

The flavour of the potatoes improves with
marinating, so this salad can be prepared in
advance. Add the herbs just before serving.

New or small potatoes 2 lb (900 g)
Dry white wine ¼ pt (150 ml)
Cider or wine vinegar 1 tbsp (15 ml)
Lemon juice 1 tbsp (15 ml)
Coarse grain French mustard 1 tbsp (15 ml)
Olive oil 6 tbsp (90 ml)
Spring onions 2
Parsley, chopped 2 tbsp (30 ml)
Salt & pepper to taste

Steam or cook the potatoes in boiling water until just
tender. Drain and as soon as possible, cut them into
thick slices.

Mix together the wine, vinegar, lemon juice,
mustard and olive oil and pour over the potatoes. Mix
well.

Thinly slice the spring onions and add to the
potatoes with the parsley. Season to taste and toss
well.

Serve warm or cold.

SPICE ISLAND SALAD

Bananas tend to discolour quickly, so make this
unusual salad just before serving.

Medium cauliflower 1
Bananas 2
Raisins 2 oz (50 g)
Mayonnaise (see p. 00) ¼ pt (150 ml)
Grated orange rind 1 tsp (5 ml)
Fresh orange juice 2 tbsp (30 ml)
Lemon juice 2 tsp (10 ml)
Ground ginger ½ tsp (2.5 ml)
Ground cinnamon ½ tsp (2.5 ml)
Salt & pepper to taste

Cut the cauliflower into small florets and just cover
with cold water. Bring to the boil then drain
immediately. Leave to go cold.

Chop the bananas and mix with the cauliflower and
raisins.

Combine the mayonnaise, orange rind and juice,
lemon juice and spices. Add to the cauliflower
mixture. Toss well and season to taste.

COTTAGE GARDEN SALAD
with apple mayonnaise

A wide range of vegetable-rennet cheeses is now available. We chose Caerphilly for this recipe, though any other hard cheese may be substituted.

White cabbage 4 oz (100 g)
Dessert apples 2
Caerphilly cheese 4 oz (100 g)
Spring onions 2
Parsley, chopped 3 tbsp (45 ml)
Apple mayonnaise (see p. 84) ¼ pt (150 ml)
Salt & pepper to taste

Finely shred the cabbage, core and dice the apples. Cube the cheese and slice the spring onions. Combine all the ingredients together, mix well and season to taste.

POPEYE SALAD

Inspired by the famous cartoon character, this salad may not give you his strength, but is undoubtedly good for you!

Young spinach leaves 4 oz (100 g)
Dried apricots, soaked overnight 2 oz (50 g)
Lentil sprouts 4 oz (100 g)
Sesame seeds, toasted 2 tbsp (30 ml)
Yoghourt & honey dressing (see p. 81) to taste
Salt & pepper to taste

Remove the coarse stalks from the spinach and shred the leaves. Chop the apricots. Combine the spinach, apricots, lentil sprouts and sesame seeds in a bowl. Toss with sufficient yoghourt and honey dressing to moisten. Season to taste.

FARMHOUSE SALAD

Many people think that beetroot should be cooked,
but it is particularly good left raw and coarsely grated.

Carrots 8 oz (225 g)
Raw beetroot 8 oz (225 g)
Onion 1 oz (25 g)
Fresh mint or dill, chopped 2 tbsp (30 ml)
Cider or wine vinegar 3 tbsp (45 ml)
Unrefined brown sugar 1 tbsp (15 ml)
Salt & pepper to taste

Coarsely grate the carrots, beetroot and onion. Mix
the mint, vinegar and sugar together. Add to the
vegetables and mix well. Season to taste.

SUNFLOWER SALAD
in an orange dressing

Carrots 8 oz (225 g)
Courgettes 8 oz (225 g)
Dried apricots, soaked overnight 2 oz (50 g)
Raisins 2 oz (50 g)
Sunflower seeds 4 tbsp (60 ml)
Orange dressing (see p. 81) ¼ pt (150 ml)
Salt & pepper to taste

Thinly slice the carrots and courgettes. Chop the
apricots. Combine all the ingredients together. Season
to taste.

GREEK SALAD

Iceberg lettuce 8 oz (225 g)
Cucumber 4 oz (100 g)
Tomatoes 4
Onion 1 oz (25 g)
Feta or goat's cheese 6 oz (175 g)
Parsley, chopped 2 tbsp (30 ml)
Fresh basil, chopped 1 tbsp (15 ml)
French dressing (see p. 79) to taste
Salt & pepper to taste

Shred the lettuce, chop the cucumber and tomatoes.
Thinly slice the onion and crumble the cheese.
Combine all the salad ingredients together. Moisten
with sufficient French dressing, toss well and season
to taste.

TROPICAL RICE SALAD
in a pineapple & sesame seed dressing

An ideal salad for a buffet, it may be prepared well
beforehand.

Long grain brown rice 6 oz (175 g)
Pineapple & sesame seed dressing (see p. 82)
¼ pt (150 ml)
Large fresh pineapple ¼
Leek 1
or *spring onions 6*
Red pepper, deseeded 1
Salt & pepper to taste

Cook the rice in boiling water for 30–35 minutes until
just tender. Drain and mix with the dressing. Leave to
go cold.

Peel the pineapple and chop, thinly slice the leek or
spring onions and the red pepper. Mix all the
ingredients together. Season to taste.

SOPHISTICATED SALAD

Try Simple lemon dressing (see p. 84) as an
alternative to French dressing for this interesting
salad.

Crisp lettuce 4 oz (100 g)
Watercress 2 oz (50 g)
Green grapes 4 oz (100 g)
Kiwi fruit 2
Cucumber 4 oz (100 g)
French dressing (see p. 79) to taste
Salt & pepper to taste

Tear the lettuce and watercress into bite sized pieces.
Remove any coarse stalks from watercress. Halve the
grapes and remove any pips. Peel the kiwi fruit and
cut each one into 8 segments. Halve the cucumber
lengthways, then cut into slices.

Mix all the salad ingredients together. Toss with
sufficient French dressing to moisten. Season to taste.

FINOCCHIO SALAD

The combination of flavour and texture makes this salad most unusual.

Potato 8 oz (225 g)
Fennel 6 oz (175 g)
Ripe pears 2
Walnuts, toasted 2 oz (50 g)
Soured cream ¼ pt (150 ml)
Lemon juice 1 tbsp (15 ml)
Watercress 2 oz (50 g)
Spring onions, chopped 6
Salt & pepper to taste

Cut the potatoes into cubes and steam or cook in boiling water for 10–15 minutes until just tender. Drain and leave to go cold.

Thinly slice the fennel. Core and dice the pears. Roughly chop the walnuts. Combine the remaining ingredients and purée in a food processor or liquidiser.

Lightly toss all the ingredients together. Season to taste.

SUCCOTASH SALAD

The use of fresh corn kernels is essential for the
perfect flavour of this salad based on an old American
Indian idea.

Fresh broad beans 1 lb (450 g)
Large corn-on-the-cob 1
Tomatoes 2
Free-range eggs, hard boiled and shelled 2
Poppy seeds 2 tsp (10 ml)
Soured cream or natural yoghourt ¼ pt (150 ml)
Onion, finely chopped 1 tbsp (15 ml)
Salt & pepper to taste

Shell the beans and cut the corn kernels from the cob.
Cook both in boiling water for about 5 minutes until
just tender. Drain and leave to go cold.

Chop the tomatoes and eggs. Combine all the
ingredients together, toss well and season to taste.

GUACAMOLE SALAD

Ripe avocados 2
Tomatoes 4
Cucumber 4 oz (100 g)
Green pepper, deseeded 1
Celery sticks 2
Onion, chopped 2 tbsp (30 ml)
Lime, juice of 1
Olive oil 4 tbsp (60 ml)
Chilli powder ½ tsp (2.5 ml)
Salt to taste

Halve, peel and remove the stones from the avocados.
Finely chop all the vegetables and mix with the lime
juice, oil, chilli powder and salt to taste.

SUMMER SALAD

Mangetout 6 oz (175 g)
Cucumber 4 oz (100 g)
Crisp lettuce 4 oz (100 g)
Spring onions 2
Double cream 6 tbsp (90 ml)
Cider or wine vinegar 4 tsp (20 ml)
Fresh tarragon, chopped 1 tbsp (15 ml)
Salt & pepper to taste

Top and tail the mangetout. Cover with boiling water,
bring back to the boil. Remove from the heat
immediately, drain and cool.

Cut the cucumber into short batons, shred the
lettuce and chop the spring onions. Mix together the
cream, vinegar and tarragon, add to the vegetables.
Mix well and season to taste.

LOLLO ROSSO SALAD

A slightly extravagant salad, but well worth it!

Lollo rosso lettuce 4 oz (100 g)
Large pineapple ¼
Avocado 1
Pine kernels, toasted 1 oz (25 g)
French dressing (see p. 79) to taste
Salt & pepper to taste

Roughly tear the lettuce leaves. Cut the pineapple into bite size pieces. Halve, peel and remove the stone from the avocado and cut into slices. Toss all the ingredients together with sufficient dressing to moisten. Season to taste.

WARM WHEATBERRY SALAD

An unusual and substantial salad, suitable to serve as a main dish.

Wholewheat berries, soaked overnight 8 oz (225 g)
Oil 4 tbsp (60 ml)
Onion, cut into rings 6 oz (175 g)
Mushrooms, wiped and sliced 8 oz (225 g)
Dill seeds 1 tsp (5 ml)
Green pepper, deseeded and sliced 1
Parsley, chopped 2 tbsp (30 ml)
Lemon juice 1 tbsp (15 ml)
Salt & pepper to taste

Drain the wholewheat berries, then cook in fresh boiling water for 30–35 minutes until just tender. Drain.

Heat the oil and sauté the onion, mushrooms and dill seeds. Add to the wheatberries with the remaining ingredients. Toss well and season to taste.

NEAPOLITAN BEAN SALAD

Flageolet beans, soaked overnight 2 oz (50 g)
Kidney beans, soaked overnight 2 oz (50 g)
Chick peas, soaked overnight 2 oz (50 g)
Green beans 4 oz (100 g)
French dressing (see p. 79) 6 tbsp (90 ml)
Celery sticks 4
Fresh chives, chopped 4 tbsp (60 ml)
Parsley, chopped 2 tbsp (30 ml)
Salt & pepper to taste

Drain the beans, then bring to the boil in fresh water.
Boil for 15 minutes, then reduce the heat and simmer
for about 50 minutes, or until tender. Drain and leave
to go cold.

Cut the green beans into bite size pieces and cook
in boiling water for about 5 minutes until tender.
Drain and leave to go cold.

Mix all the beans with the French dressing. Finely
chop the celery and add to the beans with the
chopped herbs. Season to taste and mix well.

Sophisticated Salad, page 22
Italian Salad, page 36
Drunken Potato Salad, page 15
Sunflower Salad in an Orange Dressing, page 19

Capricorn Salad, page 41
Purple Onion Salad, page 72
Louise's Salad, page 47
Citrus Salad, page 36

ORIENTAL SALAD

Fresh coconut is absolutely essential for this recipe!

Smoked tofu 8 oz (225 g)
Cucumber 4 oz (100 g)
Carrot 4 oz (100 g)
Fresh coconut 4 oz (100 g)
Beansprouts 4 oz (100 g)
French dressing (see p. 79) to taste
Salt & pepper to taste

Cut the tofu and cucumber into matchsticks. Shred the carrot and coconut coarsely. Combine all the salad ingredients. Toss with sufficient French dressing to moisten. Season to taste.

ANNIE'S SALAD

Inspired by a favourite yet curious combination of cooked beetroot and cheese originally used as a sandwich filling.

Cooked beetroot 8 oz (225 g)
Cheddar cheese 4 oz (100 g)
Onion 2 oz (50 g)
Parsley, chopped 2 tbsp (30 ml)
Orange dressing (see p. 81) to taste
Salt & pepper to taste

Cut the beetroot and Cheddar cheese into dice. Very thinly slice the onion. Combine all the ingredients with sufficient orange dressing to moisten. Season to taste.

TOASTED PEANUT SALAD

Chinese leaves or chicory 6 oz (175 g)
Radishes 6 oz (175 g)
Beansprouts 6 oz (175 g)
Peanuts, toasted 6 oz (175 g)
French dressing (see p. 79) to taste
Salt & pepper to taste

Thinly slice the Chinese leaves or chicory and the radishes. Combine with the beansprouts and peanuts. Moisten with sufficient French dressing, toss well and season to taste.

SPROUTED LENTIL SALAD

Sprouted lentils have a unique flavour reminiscent of raw peas, but if unavailable, sprouted beans may be used.

Red pepper, deseeded 1
Dessert apples 2
Lentil sprouts 4 oz (100 g)
Walnuts, toasted 2 oz (50 g)
Parsley, chopped 2 tbsp (30 ml)
French dressing (see p. 79) to taste
Salt & pepper to taste

Thinly slice the red pepper, core and dice the apples. Combine all the ingredients and moisten with sufficient French dressing. Toss well and season to taste.

OLD ENGLISH SALAD

Dessert apple 1
Cooked beetroot 8 oz (225 g)
Celery sticks 2
Walnuts, toasted 1 oz (25 g)
Watercress 1 bunch
French dressing (see p. 79) to taste
Salt & pepper to taste

Core and chop the apple. Dice the beetroot. Slice the celery and roughly chop the walnuts. Tear the watercress into bite-size pieces, removing any coarse stalks.

Combine all the ingredients with sufficient French dressing to moisten. Toss well and season to taste.

GUERNSEY TOMATO SALAD

Tomatoes 1 lb (450 g)
Spring onions 4
Walnuts, toasted 1 oz 25 g
Parsley, chopped 1 tbsp (15 ml)
French dressing (see p. 79) to taste
Salt & pepper to taste

Slice the tomatoes and arrange on a platter. Finely chop the spring onions and walnuts and sprinkle over the tomatoes with the parsley. Spoon on sufficient French dressing to moisten. Season to taste.

CAULIFLOWER, CORN & APRICOT SALAD

Baby sweetcorn 4 oz (100 g)
Cauliflower florets 6 oz (175 g)
Leek ½
Green pepper, deseeded ½
Dried apricots, soaked overnight 2 oz (50 g)
Currants 1 oz (25 g)
Yoghourt & honey dressing (see p. 81) to taste
Salt & pepper to taste

Cut the sweetcorn and the cauliflower into bite size pieces. Very thinly slice the leek and green pepper. Finely dice the apricots.

Toss all the ingredients together with sufficient dressing to moisten. Toss well and season to taste.

COTTAGE CHEESE SALAD

Cottage cheese 1 lb (450 g)
Paprika 1 tbsp (15 ml)
Spring onions 1 bunch
Celery sticks 2
Parsley, chopped 4 tbsp (60 ml)
Garlic cloves, crushed (optional) 2
French dressing (see p. 79) 2 tbsp (30 ml)
Salt & pepper to taste
Lettuce, cucumber and carrot sticks to serve

Mix together the cottage cheese and paprika. Finely chop the spring onions and celery and add to the cheese with the remaining ingredients. Mix well and season to taste. Serve on a bed of lettuce and garnish with cucumber and carrot sticks.

COLESLAW SPECIAL

Colourful and substantial, this makes an ideal
lunchtime salad.

Red cabbage 3 oz (75 g)
White cabbage 3 oz (75 g)
Carrot 1
Green pepper, deseeded ½
Leek ½
Celery sticks 2
Sunflower seeds 1 oz (25 g)
Raisins 1 oz (25 g)
French dressing (see p. 79) to taste
Salt & pepper to taste

Finely shred the cabbages. Thinly slice the carrot,
pepper, leek and celery.

Combine all the ingredients with sufficient French
dressing to moisten. Toss well and season to taste.

POLISH POTATO SALAD

Potatoes 1 lb (450 g)
Fine green beans 4 oz (100 g)
Free-range eggs, hard-boiled and shelled 4
Radishes 1 oz (25 g)
Spring onions 6
Mayonnaise (see p. 83) 6 tbsp (90 ml)
Salt & pepper to taste

Cut the potatoes into large dice and steam or cook in boiling water for about 15 minutes until tender. Drain.

Top and tail the beans and cut in half. Steam or cook in boiling water for 3–4 minutes until just tender. Drain.

Roughly chop the eggs. Slice the radishes and spring onions. Combine all the salad ingredients together. Mix with the mayonnaise and season to taste.

ITALIAN SALAD

Wholemeal pasta shapes 4 oz (100 g)
French dressing (see p. 79) 6 tbsp (90 ml)
Courgettes 2
Leek 1
Tomatoes 2
Black olives, pitted 2 oz (50 g)
Salt & pepper to taste

Cook the pasta in boiling water for about 15 minutes, or until just tender. Drain and mix with the French dressing.

Thinly slice the courgettes and leek, chop the tomatoes and olives. Add to the pasta, toss well and season to taste.

CITRUS SALAD

Large grapefruit or oranges 2
Spring onions 4
Baby sweetcorn 8 oz (225 g)
Beansprouts 8 oz (225 g)
Cashew nuts, toasted 4 oz (100 g)
Pineapple & sesame seed dressing (see p. 82) to taste
Salt & pepper to taste

Peel the grapefruit or oranges, discarding all the white pith. Cut the fruit into segments. Chop the spring onions. Cut the sweetcorn into bite size pieces.

Combine all the salad ingredients, toss with sufficient dressing to moisten. Season to taste.

WINTER ROOT SALAD

These crunchy winter vegetables are all the more tasty
in this unusual soured cream dressing.

Parsnip 4 oz (100 g)
Carrot 4 oz (100 g)
Swede 4 oz (100 g)
Soured cream ¼ pt (150 ml)
Coarse grain mustard 1 tsp (5 ml)
Cider or wine vinegar 1 tsp (5 ml)
Poppy seeds ½ tsp (2.5 ml)
Salt & pepper to taste

Coarsely grate the vegetables. Mix the soured cream
with the remaining ingredients. Add to the vegetables,
season to taste and mix well.

SPROUTING SALAD

Try sprouting your own seeds for this salad. They are tasty, nutritious and full of vitamins.

Crisp lettuce 8 oz (225 g)
Leek 1
Alfalfa sprouts 3 oz (75 g)
Lentil sprouts 2 oz (50 g)
Mustard and cress 1 carton
Mayonnaise (see p. 83) ¼ pt (150 ml)
Lime, grated rind and juice of 1
Salt & pepper to taste

Shred the lettuce, finely slice the leek.

Combine all the salad ingredients in a bowl. Mix the mayonnaise with the rind and juice of the lime. Add to the salad, toss well and season to taste.

AROMATIC AUBERGINE SALAD

The flavour of this salad is improved by cooking the basic mixture well in advance and leaving it up to 24 hours to marinate before adding the remaining ingredients.

Medium aubergine 1
Small onion 1
Oil 3 tbsp (45 ml)
Curry powder 1 tsp (5 ml)
Lemon 1
Tomatoes 8 oz (225 g)
Green pepper, deseeded ½
Salt to taste
Fresh coriander, chopped 2 tbsp (30 ml)

Cut the aubergine into dice. Cover with water and bring to the boil. Drain well.

Cut the onion into thin rings. Heat the oil and sauté the aubergine and onion with the curry powder until just tender. Remove from the heat and transfer to a bowl, adding the pan juices. Finely grate the rind from half the lemon and squeeze the juice from both halves. Add to the aubergine and leave to cool.

Chop the tomatoes and green pepper. Stir into the aubergine and season generously with salt. Sprinkle with chopped coriander.

CUCUMBER COOL

A perfect cooling side salad to accompany a hot main course.

Cucumber 1
Salt 2 tsp (10 ml)
Water ¼ pt (150 ml)
Unrefined brown sugar 2 tbsp (30 ml)
Cider or wine vinegar 2 tbsp (30 ml)
Chilli powder a pinch

Thinly slice the cucumber, sprinkle with salt and leave for 30 minutes. Rinse and drain well.

Place the water and sugar in a saucepan. Heat gently to dissolve, then remove from the heat and add the vinegar and chilli powder to taste. Pour over the cucumber. Cover and leave to marinate for several hours.

VIENNESE SALAD
with apple mayonnaise

Red cabbage 6 oz (175 g)
Dessert apple 1
Raisins 1 oz (25 g)
Caraway seeds ½ tsp (2.5 ml)
Apple mayonnaise (see p. 84) 6 tbsp (90 ml)
Salt & pepper to taste

Finely shred the cabbage. Core and chop the apple. Mix all the ingredients together, toss well and season to taste.

CAPRICORN SALAD

An ideal salad starter for a dinner party – Capricorn is a creamy English goat's cheese with a mellow flavour.

Lollo rosso or oak leaf lettuce 4 oz (100 g)
Iceberg lettuce 4 oz (100 g)
Green grapes 4 oz (100 g)
Capricorn goat's cheese 4 oz (100 g)
Wholemeal bread 4 oz (100 g)
Butter 1 oz (25 g)
Oil 2 tbsp (30 ml)
French dressing (see p. 79) to taste
Salt & pepper to taste

Tear the lettuce into bite size pieces. Halve the green grapes and remove the pips. Dice the cheese. Remove the crusts from the bread and cut into batons. Heat the butter and oil and fry the bread batons until crisp and golden. Drain on absorbent paper.

Just before serving, toss all the ingredients together with sufficient French dressing to moisten. Season to taste.

PINEAPPLE & PEPPER SLAW

White cabbage 4 oz (100 g)
Celery 4 oz (100 g)
Red pepper, deseeded 1
Large pineapple ¼
Mayonnaise (see p. 83) 5 tbsp (75 ml)
Salt & pepper to taste

Finely shred the cabbage and slice the celery. Cut the red pepper into thin slices. Peel the pineapple and chop.

Combine all the ingredients together, toss well and season to taste.

PROVENÇALE SALAD

Look out for this delicate, pale green cauliflower which has recently appeared in the shops!

Speciality green cauliflower 12 oz (350 g)
Black olives, pitted 2 oz (50 g)
Tomatoes 2
French dressing (see p. 79) 5 tbsp (75 ml)
Tomato purée 1 tbsp (15 ml)
Fresh basil, chopped 1 tbsp (15 ml)
Salt & pepper to taste

Cut the cauliflower into florets. Cover with water and just bring to the boil. Drain well.

Slice the olives, chop the tomatoes. Mix the French dressing with the tomato purée. Mix all the salad ingredients together. Toss well in the dressing, add the basil and season to taste.

GOLDEN RAIN SALAD

Long grain brown rice 4 oz (100 g)
French dressing (see p. 79) to taste
Corn-on-the-cob 1
Yellow pepper, deseeded ½
Onion 1 oz (25 g)
Yellow marigold or nasturtium flowers 4
Salt & pepper to taste

Cook the rice in boiling water for 30–35 minutes until just tender. Drain well and toss with sufficient French dressing to moisten.

Cut the corn kernels from the cob and cook in boiling water for 5 minutes. Drain and add to the rice. Leave to cool.

Finely dice the yellow pepper and onion. Pluck the petals from the marigolds and add to the rice with the diced vegetables. If wished, nasturtium flowers may be added whole to the salad.

Toss with extra French dressing to taste. Season generously.

POTATO AND CUCUMBER SALAD
with mustard mayonnaise

So simple and yet so delicious!

Small new potatoes 1 lb (450 g)
Large cucumber ¼
Mustard mayonnaise (see p. 84) ¼ pt (150 ml)
Salt & pepper to taste

Cook the potatoes whole in boiling water for about 15 minutes until just tender. Drain and leave to cool.

Cut the cucumber in half lengthways and remove the seeds, then slice the cucumber thickly.

Combine the ingredients together and toss well. Season to taste.

Marinated Mushrooms, page 67
Christmas Salad, page 60
Sunset Salad, page 55

Aromatic Aubergine Salad, page 39
Mediterranean Salad, page 69
Spicy Potato Salad in a Curry Dressing, page 12
Mixed Leaf Salad, page 56

MARINATED PEPPERS WITH GARLIC

Best made one to two days ahead to develop the flavour.

Large yellow pepper 1
Large red pepper 1
Large green pepper 1
Garlic cloves 2
Olive oil 4 tbsp (60 ml)
Cider or wine vinegar 1 tbsp (15 ml)
Salt & pepper to taste

Cut the peppers into quarters, discard the stalks and seeds. Cut each pepper quarter into 4 long strips. Cut the garlic into thin slices. Heat the oil and sauté the garlic until lightly brown. Add the pepper strips and cook over gentle heat, stirring occasionally for about 20 minutes until tender. Remove from the heat, add the vinegar and season generously. Leave to cool.

FRUIT & NUT SALAD

Celery sticks 4
Dessert apples 2
Walnuts, toasted 2 oz (50 g)
Dried apricots 2 oz (50 g)
Raisins 2 oz (50 g)
French dressing (see p. 79) to taste
Salt & pepper to taste

Thinly slice the celery, core and dice the apples. Chop the walnuts and dried apricots.

Toss all the ingredients together with sufficient French dressing to moisten. Season to taste.

LOUISE'S SALAD

A salad inspired for those who dislike vegetables!

Kidney beans, soaked overnight 4 oz (100 g)
Long grain brown rice 6 oz (175 g)
French dressing (see p. 79) to taste
Currants 2 oz (50 g)
Sultanas 2 oz (50 g)
Peanuts, toasted 2 oz (50 g)
Poppy seeds 1 tbsp (15 ml)
Sesame seeds, toasted 1 tbsp (15 ml)
Salt & pepper to taste

Drain the beans, then bring to the boil in fresh water. Boil for 15 minutes, then reduce heat and simmer for about 50 minutes or until tender. Drain.

Cook the rice in boiling water for 30–35 minutes or until just tender. Drain.

Toss the beans and rice with sufficient French dressing to moisten. Leave to cool.

Combine all the ingredients together, adding extra dressing if required. Toss well and season to taste.

SPANISH SALAD

Ideal for a starter!

Medium oranges 4
Black olives, pitted 12
Onion, finely chopped 2 tbsp (30 ml)
Parsley, finely chopped 2 tbsp (30 ml)
French dressing (see p. 79) to taste

Peel the oranges, using a small serrated knife to remove all the white pith. Thinly slice the fruit and arrange on a plate.

Finely chop the olives and scatter over the oranges with the onion and parsley. Moisten with sufficient French dressing to taste.

LITTLE GEMS WITH SOFT CHEESE DRESSING

An easy salad perfect for a party food.

Little gem lettuce 4
Soft cheese dressing (see p. 82) ⅓ pt (200 ml)

Cut the lettuce into quarters. Arrange on a plate and drizzle the dressing over just before serving.

BROCCOLI & TOFU SALAD
in a ginger dressing

A high protein salad with an oriental influence.

Firm tofu 5 oz (150 g)
Ginger dressing (see p. 81) ¼ pt (150 ml)
Aduki beans, soaked overnight 4 oz (100 g)
Broccoli 8 oz (225 g)
Whole almonds, toasted 2 oz (50 g)
Soya sauce 1 tbsp (15 ml)
Salt & pepper to taste

Cut the tofu into thick batons. Pour the ginger dressing over, cover and leave to marinate.

Drain the beans, then bring to the boil in fresh water. Boil for 10 minutes, then reduce the heat and simmer for 30–40 minutes until tender. Drain well and leave to cool.

Cut the broccoli heads into florets and dice the stalk. Cover with boiling water in a small saucepan and bring back to the boil. Drain well and leave to cool.

Mix together the beans, broccoli, almonds and soya sauce. Carefully add the tofu and dressing. Mix well and season to taste.

SLIMMERS' SALAD

Carrots 8 oz (225 g)
Red skinned dessert apple 1
Seedless green grapes 4 oz (100 g)
Sunflower seeds 2 tbsp (30 ml)
Lemon juice 1 tbsp (15 ml)
Salt & pepper to taste

Very thinly slice the carrots. Core and chop the apple. Mix together with the grapes and sunflower seeds.

Mix the lemon juice with 2 tbsp (30 ml) water and pour over the salad. Season generously and toss well.

PASTA VERDE SALAD

Wholewheat macaroni 4 oz (100 g)
French dressing (see p. 79) to taste
Large courgette 1
Leek ½
Green pepper, deseeded ½
Sesame seeds, toasted 2 tbsp (30 ml)
Parsley, chopped 2 tbsp (30 ml)
Salt & pepper to taste

Cook the macaroni according to packet directions. Drain well, toss in sufficient French dressing to moisten. Leave to cool.

Very thinly slice the courgette and leek. Finely dice the green pepper. Add the vegetables to the pasta with the sesame seeds and parsley. Toss well, adding extra dressing if wished. Season to taste.

MEXICAN BEAN SALAD
in a chilli dressing

Pinto beans, soaked overnight 4 oz (100 g)
Chilli dressing (see p. 80) to taste
Celery sticks 4
Small red pepper, deseeded 1
Avocado 1

Drain the beans and bring to the boil in fresh water.
Boil for 10 minutes, then reduce the heat and simmer
for about 50 minutes until tender. Drain well and toss
in sufficient dressing to moisten. Leave to cool.

Finely slice the celery and dice the red pepper. Add
to the beans and mix well, adding more dressing if
wished.

Just before serving, halve, peel and remove the
stone from the avocado. Dice and add to the salad.
Toss gently.

POTATO SALAD WITH FRESH DILL

Potatoes 1½ lb (675 g)
Spring onions 2
Fresh dill, chopped 3 tbsp (45 ml)
Mayonnaise (see p. 83) or *soured cream ¼ pt (150 ml)*
French mustard 1 tbsp (15 ml)
Cider or wine vinegar 1 tsp (5 ml)
Salt & pepper to taste

Steam or cook the potatoes in boiling water for about 20 minutes until just tender. Drain well and chop roughly.

Finely chop the spring onion. Combine with the dill, mayonnaise or soured cream, mustard and vinegar. Mix well and add to the potatoes. Toss carefully and season to taste.

PLUM SALAD

This unusual salad was inspired by an overloaded plum tree!

Ripe plums 1 lb (450 g)
Celery stick 1
Spring onion 1
French dressing (see p. 79) to taste
Salt & pepper to taste

Halve, stone and slice the plums. Finely dice the celery and onion.

Toss all the ingredients together carefully with sufficient French dressing to moisten. Season to taste.

"BREAD" SALAD

Flageolet beans, soaked overnight 3 oz (75 g)
Cucumber ½
Tomatoes 4
Spring onions 8
Crisp lettuce, spinach or sorrel 4 oz (100 g)
Parsley, chopped 4 tbsp (60 ml)
Fresh mint, chopped 2 tbsp (30 ml)
Wholemeal bread 4 oz (100 g)
Olive oil 2 tbsp (30 ml)
Lemon juice 1 tbsp (15 ml)
Natural yoghourt 4 fl oz (100 ml)
Garlic clove, crushed 1
Salt & pepper to taste

Drain the beans, then bring to the boil in fresh water.
Boil for 10 minutes, reduce the heat and simmer for
about 50 minutes or until tender. Drain and cool.

Finely chop the cucumber, tomatoes and spring
onions. Shred the lettuce. Dice and toast the bread
until crisp.

Mix the remaining ingredients together for the
dressing. Combine the beans, cucumber, tomatoes,
lettuce, herbs and dressing. Season to taste.

Just before serving, add the toasted bread cubes.

ROSY RICE SALAD

Long grain brown rice 4 oz (100 g)
Garlic dressing (see p. 80) to taste
Small onion (red) ½
Red pepper, deseeded ½
Tomatoes 8 oz (225 g)
Parsley, chopped 3 tbsp (45 ml)
Salt & pepper to taste

Cook the rice in boiling water for 30–35 minutes until just tender. Drain well. Mix with sufficient garlic dressing to moisten. Leave to cool.

Finely chop the onion and roughly chop the pepper and tomatoes.

Combine all the ingredients, adding extra dressing if necessary. Toss well and season to taste.

SUNSET SALAD

Redcurrants have a short season, so a good alternative
for winter is pomegranate seeds.

Carrots 6 oz (175 g)
Red skinned dessert apples 2
Redcurrants 6 oz (175 g)
Hazelnuts, toasted 1½ oz (40 g)
French dressing (see p. 79) to taste
Salt & pepper to taste

Top and tail the carrots, then using a potato peeler,
shred them into ribbons. Core and dice the apples.
Top and tail the redcurrants.

Combine all the salad ingredients with sufficient
French dressing to moisten. Toss carefully and season
to taste.

AMERICAN FRUIT SALAD

Ideal for a salad starter.

Large melon ½
Oranges 2
Tomatoes 1 lb (450 g)
Salt & pepper to taste
Chantilly mayonnaise (see p. 83) ⅓ pt (200 ml)

Remove the seeds and rind from the melon. Using a small serrated knife, cut the skin and pith from the oranges. Roughly chop the fruit and tomatoes and mix together. Season to taste.

Either serve with Chantilly mayonnaise separately or mix into the salad just before serving.

MIXED LEAF SALAD

As a variation to this salad add several edible flower heads or petals such as clover, pansy, carnation, nasturtium, rose or borage.

Assorted salad leaves, such as lollo rosso, escarole, radicchio,
quattro stagioni 8 oz (225 g)
Garlic dressing (see p. 80) ¼ pt (150 ml)
Salt & pepper to taste

Wash the salad leaves and thoroughly dry them. Tear the leaves into bite size pieces.

Just before serving, toss with the dressing to coat all the leaves. Season to taste.

BULGHAR & CUMIN SEED SALAD

Bulghar wheat 8 oz (225 g)
Red pepper, deseeded 1
Green pepper, deseeded 1
Black olives, pitted 4 oz (100 g)
Cumin seeds 1 tsp (5 ml)
Garlic dressing (see p. 80) ¼ pt (150 ml)
Turmeric ½ tsp (2.5 ml)
Salt & pepper to taste

Wash the bulghar wheat, then just cover with boiling water and leave to soak for 30 minutes. Drain well and squeeze out excess water.

Finely dice the peppers. Slice the olives.

Cook the cumin seeds in a heavy based pan until they change colour and start to pop. Add to the dressing with the turmeric.

Toss all the ingredients together. Season to taste.

WINTER SLAW
with yoghourt mayonnaise

Brussels sprouts 4 oz (100 g)
Carrot 4 oz (100 g)
Celery sticks 4
Pumpkin seeds 1 oz (25 g)
Raisins 2 oz (50 g)
Mayonnaise (see p. 83) 5 tbsp (75 ml)
Natural yoghourt 5 tbsp (75 ml)
Salt & pepper to taste

Finely shred the Brussels sprouts, carrot and celery.
Toss the salad ingredients in a bowl. Mix the
mayonnaise and yoghourt.

Toss all the ingredients together and season to taste.

AMERICAN WALDORF SALAD

Celery sticks 6
Dessert apples 2
Green grapes 4 oz (100 g)
Pecan nuts, toasted 2 oz (50 g)
Mayonnaise (see p. 83) ¼ pt (150 ml)
Salt & pepper to taste

Roughly chop the celery and core and chop the
apples. Halve the grapes and remove the pips. Toss all
the ingredients together and season to taste.

CELERIAC REMOULADE

Medium celeriac 1½–1¾ lb (675–800 g)
Mustard mayonnaise (see p. 84) ½ pt (300 ml)
Celery seeds 1 tsp (5 ml)
Parsley, chopped 4 tbsp (60 ml)
Salt & pepper to taste

Peel the celeriac if necessary and cut it into very thin batons. Place in a saucepan of boiling water and bring just back to the boil. Drain immediately and drop into iced water. Leave to go cold. Drain well and dry thoroughly.

Toss all the ingredients together and season to taste.

CHRISTMAS SALAD

Chestnuts 8 oz (225 g)
Brussels sprouts 8 oz (225 g)
Tangerines 3
Spring onions 6
Fresh sage leaves 12
French dressing (see p. 79) to taste
Salt & pepper to taste

Cut a cross on the flat side of each chestnut. Place in a saucepan, cover with water and bring to the boil. Boil for 5 minutes, drain and remove the shells. Return to the pan, cover with water and bring to the boil. Boil for 5 minutes, drain and leave to cool. Remove the skins and roughly chop the chestnuts.

Finely shred the Brussels sprouts. Using a small serrated knife remove the skin and pith from the tangerines. Roughly chop the fruit. Chop the spring onions.

Combine all the ingredients with sufficient French dressing to moisten. Season to taste.

Coleslaw Special, page 34
Warm Wheatberry Salad, page 27
Popeye Salad, page 18
Spanish Salad, page 48

Neapolitan Bean Salad, page 28
Annie's Salad, page 29
Toasted Peanut Salad, page 30

AUTUMN SALAD

Green lentils, soaked overnight 2 oz (50 g)
Carrot 2 oz (50 g)
Courgette 2 oz (50 g)
Celery sticks 2
Assorted salad leaves such as escarole, oakleaf, radicchio,
lollo rosso
Garlic dressing (see p. 80) to taste
Salt & pepper to taste

Drain the lentils then bring to the boil in fresh water. Reduce the heat, cover and simmer for 10–15 minutes until tender. Drain well and leave to cool.

Cut the carrot, courgette and celery into batons. Tear the salad leaves into bite size pieces. Place all the ingredients in a bowl. Just before serving, toss with sufficient garlic dressing to coat all the leaves. Season to taste.

VEGETABLE SALAD

Medium celeriac ½ (12–14 oz) (350–400 g)
New potatoes, cooked 1 lb (450 g)
Carrot 4 oz (100 g)
Green pepper, deseeded 1
Onion, chopped 2 tbsp (30 ml)
Mayonnaise (see p. 83) ⅓ pt (200 ml)
Salt & pepper to taste

Peel the celeriac if necessary and cut into very thin batons. Place in a saucepan of boiling water and bring just back to the boil. Drain immediately and drop into iced water. Leave to go cold. Drain well and dry thoroughly.

Cut the potatoes into chunks. Cut the carrot into batons. Dice the pepper. Combine all the salad ingredients together with the mayonnaise. Toss well and season to taste.

MELON & ALMOND SALAD

Look out for orange peppers to enhance the colour of
this lovely starter salad.

Large melon ½
Orange pepper, deseeded 1
Celery sticks 4
Flaked almonds, toasted 2 oz (50 g)
Orange & honey dressing (see p. 85) ¼ pt (150 ml)
Salt & pepper to taste

Remove the seeds and rind from the melon and dice
the fruit. Dice the pepper and slice the celery.

Combine all the ingredients together. Toss well and
season to taste.

SOYA BEANSPROUT SALAD

Soya beansprouts 10 oz (300 g)
Leek 1
Cauliflower florets 8 oz (225 g)
Green pepper, deseeded 1
Orange & honey dressing (see p. 85) ⅓ pt (200 ml)
Salt & pepper to taste

Soak the soya beansprouts in cold water for 5 minutes. Drain well and dry thoroughly. Finely shred the leek. Cut the cauliflower florets into bite size pieces and dice the pepper.

Combine all the ingredients together, toss well with the dressing and season to taste.

SPROUTED MUNG BEAN SALAD
in an orange and honey dressing

Beansprouts 10 oz (300 g)
Carrots 8 oz (225 g)
Radishes 3 oz (75 g)
Green pepper, deseeded 1
Mustard and cress 1 carton
Orange & honey dressing (see p. 85) ⅓ pt (200 ml)
Salt & pepper to taste

Soak the beansprouts in cold water for 5 minutes. Drain well and dry thoroughly. Finely slice the carrots and radishes. Dice the green pepper.

Combine all the ingredients together, toss well with the dressing and season to taste.

JERUSALEM ARTICHOKE SALAD

Jerusalem artichokes 1 lb (450 g)
Lemon juice 2 tbsp (30 ml)
Tomatoes 1 lb (450 g)
Mayonnaise (see p. 83) 5 tbsp (75 ml)
Single cream 5 tbsp (75 ml)
Coarse grain mustard 1 tbsp (15 ml)
Parsley, chopped 2 tbsp (30 ml)
Salt & pepper to taste

Scrub the artichokes. Place in a saucepan and just cover with cold water. Add half the lemon juice and bring to the boil. Reduce the heat and simmer for about 15 minutes until just tender. Drain well and leave to cool.

Roughly chop the tomatoes and artichokes.

Combine all the remaining ingredients, except the parsley, to make the dressing. Season to taste.

Arrange the artichokes and tomatoes in a shallow dish, sprinkle with parsley and drizzle with the mustard dressing.

SWEET & SOUR COURGETTES

A delicious starter salad which can be prepared the day before.

Small courgettes 1 lb (450 g)
Garlic cloves 2
Oil 3 tbsp (45 ml)
Cider or wine vinegar 3 tbsp (45 ml)
Water 3 tbsp (45 ml)
Raisins 2 tbsp (30 ml)
Pine nuts, toasted 2 tbsp (30 ml)
Salt & pepper to taste

Cut the courgettes lengthways into thin slices. Thinly slice the garlic. Heat the oil and lightly sauté the courgettes and garlic. Add the remaining ingredients and bring to the boil. Remove from the heat, transfer to a bowl. Leave to cool.

Season to taste and toss well before serving.

MARINATED MUSHROOMS

Try to use the brown skinned chestnut mushrooms
for this salad as they have a strong, distinctive flavour.

Mushroom caps 1 lb (450 g)
Olive oil 8 tbsp (120 ml)
Lemon juice 4 tbsp (60 ml)
Onion, finely chopped 4 tbsp (60 ml)
Fresh chives, chopped 2 tbsp (30 ml)
Parsley, chopped 2 tbsp (30 ml)
Salt & pepper to taste

Wipe the mushrooms and quarter. Place in a bowl
with the oil, lemon juice and onion and season
generously. Cover and leave for 1–2 hours in a cool
place.

Add the herbs and season to taste.

FRESH BEAN SALAD

A particularly good salad to serve with a main dish.

Green beans 8 oz (225 g)
Mangetout 4 oz (100 g)
Shelled broad beans 4 oz (100 g)
Garlic dressing (see p. 80) ¼ pt (150 ml)
Salt & pepper to taste

Top and tail the beans and mangetout. Cut the beans into bite size pieces. Place all the beans in boiling water, bring back to the boil and simmer for 2–3 minutes until just tender. Drain and cool.

Place the mangetout in boiling water and bring just back to the boil. Drain immediately. Leave to cool.

Toss all the ingredients together and season to taste.

MEDITERRANEAN SALAD

Small okra 1 lb (450 g)
Small onion 1
Dried apricots 3 oz (75 g)
Tomatoes 8 oz (225 g)
Oil 2 tbsp (30 ml)
Garlic dressing (see p. 80) ¼ pt (150 ml)
Cumin seeds, toasted 1 tsp (5 ml)
Turmeric ½ tsp (2.5 ml)
Dried basil ½ tsp (2.5 ml)
Salt & pepper to taste

Top and tail the okra as necessary. Thinly slice the onion. Cut the apricot into strips and dice the tomato. Heat the oil and sauté the okra and onion for 7–10 minutes until just tender. Leave to cool.

Transfer to a bowl and add the remaining ingredients. Cover and leave in a cool place for several hours.

Toss well and season to taste.

COOKED VEGETABLE SALAD

Fine green beans 4 oz (100 g)
Carrot 4 oz (100 g)
Shelled peas 4 oz (100 g)
Cucumber 4 oz (100 g)
Natural yoghourt ½ pt (300 ml)
Ground cumin ½ tsp (2.5 ml)
Paprika ½ tsp (2.5 ml)
Parsley, chopped 2 tbsp (30 ml)
Salt & pepper to taste

Cut the beans and carrots into small dice. Place in a saucepan of boiling water with the peas and cook for 3–4 minutes until just tender. Drain and cool.

Dice the cucumber and add to the vegetables.

Combine the remaining ingredients, add to the vegetables. Toss well and season to taste.

EASTERN SALAD
in a spicy peanut dressing

Baby sweetcorn 1 lb (450 g)
Cucumber 8 oz (225 g)
Spicy peanut dressing (see p. 85) ¼ pt (150 ml)

Cut the sweetcorn in half if wished. Quarter the cucumber lengthways, remove the seeds and slice thickly.

Combine the sweetcorn and cucumber with the dressing. Toss well.

ITALIAN DRESSED BROCCOLI

Broccoli 1 lb (450 g)
Carrots 4 oz (100 g)
Olive oil 4 tbsp (60 ml)
Lemon juice 2 tbsp (30 ml)
Dried chilli, crumbled 1
Salt to taste

Cut the broccoli into florets and quarter the stalks and cut into 1 in (2.5 cm) pieces. Cut the carrots into batons. Place the broccoli and carrots in boiling water. Bring back to the boil. Drain immediately and leave to cool.

Toss all the ingredients together. Cover and leave to marinate for at least 1 hour. Season to taste.

LEEKS IN AVOCADO DRESSING

Young leeks 2 lb (900 g)
Vegetable stock 1 pt (600 ml)
Avocado dressing (see p. 80) ½ pt (300 ml)
Salt & pepper to taste

Cut the leeks into 1 in (2.5 cm) lengths. Place in a wide, shallow pan and cover with boiling stock. Cook for 5 minutes. Drain immediately and leave to cool.

Toss with avocado dressing and season to taste.

PURPLE ONION SALAD

Purple onion 8 oz (225 g)
Unrefined brown sugar 2 oz (50 g)
Salt 1 tsp (5 ml)
Cider or wine vinegar 2 tbsp (30 ml)
Water 2 tbsp (30 ml)
Radicchio 4 oz (100 g)
Black grapes 8 oz (225 g)
Sunflower seeds 2 tbsp (30ml)
Lemon & honey dressing (see p. 85) ¼ pt (150 ml)

Thinly slice the onions and mix with the next four ingredients. Leave to marinate for 1 hour, then drain and squeeze out excess moisture.

Tear the radicchio into bite size pieces. Halve and remove the pips from the grapes. Mix together the onion, radicchio, grapes and sunflower seeds and toss with the dressing.

MUSHROOM & ALMOND SALAD

Button mushrooms 1 lb (450 g)
Oil 2 tbsp (30 ml)
Curry powder 1 tsp (5 ml)
Lemon juice 1 tsp (5 ml)
Mayonnaise (see p. 83) ¼ pt (150 ml)
Almonds, toasted 2 oz (50 g)
Salt & pepper to taste

Wipe the mushrooms, thickly slice and sauté in the oil with the curry powder until just evenly coloured. Remove from the heat, add the lemon juice and leave to cool.

Stir in the mayonnaise and almonds. Season to taste.

PARSNIP, CELERY & APPLE SALAD

Medium parsnips 2
Celery heart 8 oz (225 g)
Dessert apples 2
Lemon & honey dressing (see p. 85) ⅓ pt (200 ml)
Salt & pepper to taste

Finely grate the parsnips, thinly slice the celery and core and dice the apples.

Mix together with the dressing, toss well and season to taste.

SPINACH & ORANGE SALAD

Young spinach leaves 4 oz (100 g)
Oranges 2
Carrots 6 oz (175 g)
Sultanas 2 oz (50 g)
Poppy seeds 1 tbsp (15 ml)
Tofu & yoghourt dressing or *Orange & honey dressing (see*
p. 86 and p. 85) ¼ pt (150 ml)
Salt & pepper to taste

Shred the spinach into bite size pieces. Using a
serrated knife, peel the oranges, removing all the
white pith. Cut the oranges into quarters and slice
each quarter thickly. Finely grate the carrots.

Combine all the ingredients together, toss well and
season to taste.

WATERCRESS & YELLOW TOMATO SALAD

If yellow tomatoes are not available, use cherry tomatoes instead.

Watercress 1 bunch
Cucumber ½
Yellow tomatoes 1 lb (450 g)
Mint dressing (see p. 81) to taste
Salt & pepper to taste

Wash and dry the watercress well and roughly chop. Dice the cucumber and quarter the tomatoes.

Mix the salad ingredients together, then toss with sufficient dressing to just moisten the leaves. Season to taste.

RATATOUILLE SALAD

Serve this as a snack meal with garlic bread.

Onion 4 oz (100 g)
Garlic cloves 2
Aubergine 8 oz (225 g)
Courgettes 8 oz (225 g)
Red pepper, deseeded 1
Tomatoes 8 oz (225 g)
Olive oil 4 tbsp (60 ml)
Tomato purée 2 tbsp (30 ml)
Fresh thyme sprigs a few
Parsley, chopped 1 tbsp (15 ml)
Fresh basil leaves, sliced 12
Lemon juice 1 tbsp (15 ml)
Salt & pepper to taste

Cut the vegetables into medium slices. Heat the oil and sauté the onion until transparent. Add the aubergine and sauté for 2–3 minutes. Add the courgettes, pepper and tomatoes. Sauté for 5 minutes. Add the tomato purée and fresh thyme. Reduce heat, cover and simmer very gently for 20 minutes, stirring occasionally.

Leave to cool, then stir in the remaining ingredients and season to taste.

Lollo Rosso Salad, page 26
Golden Rain Salad, page 43
Broccoli and Tofu Salad in a Ginger Dressing, page 49

Cottage Cheese Salad, page 33
Cucumber Cool, page 40
Pineapple & Pepper Slaw, page 42
Little Gems with Soft Cheese Dressing, page 48

ITALIAN RISOTTO SALAD

An authentic Italian risotto adapted to make a superb
salad.

Dried ceps ¾ oz (20 g)
Shallots 2
Butter 1 oz (25 g)
Brown risotto rice 8 oz (225 g)
Dry white wine ¼ pt (150 ml)
Saffron threads, a generous pinch
Vegetable stock cube 1
Button mushrooms 4 oz (100 g)
Shelled peas, cooked 4 oz (100 g)
Parmesan cheese, grated 1 oz (25 g)
French dressing (see p. 79) to taste
Salt & pepper to taste

Cover the ceps with boiling water and leave for at
least 30 minutes. Drain and reserve the liquid. Make
up to ¾ pt (450 ml) with water.

Finely chop the shallots. Melt the butter and sauté
the shallots. Add the rice and cook, stirring until the
rice becomes translucent. Add the white wine, saffron
threads, ceps, the reserved liquid and the stock cube.
Simmer covered for 30–35 minutes, stirring
occasionally until the rice is tender and all the liquid is
absorbed. Add a little extra water if necessary. Wipe
and slice the button mushrooms, add to the rice.
Leave to cool.

Add the cooked peas, cheese and sufficient French
dressing to moisten. Toss well and season to taste.

ORIENTAL SALAD
in a tangy apricot dressing

Lettuce 4 oz (100 g)
Water chestnuts, canned 8 oz (225 g)
Soya beansprouts 8 oz (225 g)
Almonds, toasted 4 oz (100 g)
Tangy apricot dressing (see p. 86) ⅓ pt (200 ml)
Salt & pepper to taste

Tear the lettuce into bite size pieces. Slice the water chestnuts.

Combine the salad ingredients and toss with the dressing. Season to taste.

FRENCH DRESSING

This recipe forms the basis of a number of Cranks dressings. It can be varied in many ways by the addition of extra ingredients (see following pages). For a thinner dressing, add a little water when blending.

Lemon, juice of 2
Cider or wine vinegar 4 tbsp (60 ml)
Salt 1½ tsp (7.5 ml)
Pepper ½ tsp (2.5 ml)
French mustard 1 tbsp (15 ml)
Unrefined brown sugar 2 tsp (10 ml)
Oil ¾ pt (450 ml)

Put the lemon juice, vinegar, salt, pepper, mustard and sugar in a jug. Whisk with a fork until evenly blended, then slowly work in the oil. Store in a refrigerator.

OR

Put all the ingredients together in a liquidiser goblet and blend for a few seconds.

OR

Shake all the ingredients together in a screw top jar.

Makes about 1 pt (600 ml).

AVOCADO DRESSING

Ripe avocado, chopped ½
French dressing ¼ pt (150 ml)
Iced water 5 tbsp (75 ml)

Blend the ingredients together in a liquidiser.

Makes about 12 fl oz (350 ml).

CHILLI DRESSING

French dressing ½ pt (300 ml)
Chilli powder or *tobasco to taste*

Mix ingredients together to taste.

Makes about ½ pt (300 ml).

CURRY DRESSING

French dressing ¼ pt (150 ml)
Curry powder 1½ tsp (7.5 ml)
Turmeric ½ tsp (2.5 ml)

Mix all the ingredients together.

Makes about ¼ pt (150 ml).

GARLIC DRESSING

French dressing ½ pt (300 ml)
Garlic cloves, crushed 2

Mix the ingredients together.

Makes about ½ pt (300 ml).

GINGER DRESSING

French dressing ½ pt (300 ml)
Root ginger, finely grated 1 tbsp (15 ml)

Mix all the ingredients together.

Makes about ½ pt (300 ml).

MINT DRESSING

French dressing ½ pt (300 ml)
Fresh mint chopped 3 tbsp (45 ml)
or dried mint 1 tbsp (15 ml)

Mix the ingredients together.

Makes about ½ pt (300 ml).

ORANGE DRESSING

French dressing ⅓ pt (200 ml)
Fresh orange juice 3 fl oz (90 ml)

Mix the ingredients together.

Makes about ½ pt (300 ml).

YOGHOURT & HONEY DRESSING

French dressing ¼ pt (150 ml)
Natural yoghourt ¼ pt (150 ml)
Honey 1 tbsp (15 ml)

Mix all the ingredients together.

Makes about ½ pt (300 ml).

PINEAPPLE & SESAME SEED DRESSING

French dressing 6 fl oz (175 ml)
Pineapple juice 3 fl oz (90 ml)
Soya sauce 1 fl oz (25 ml)
Sesame seeds, toasted 1 tbsp (15 ml)
Ground ginger 1 tsp (5 ml)

Mix all the ingredients together.

Makes about ½ pt (300 ml).

SOFT CHEESE DRESSING

French dressing ¼ pt (150 ml)
Soft cheese 4 oz (100 g)
Water 3 tbsp (45 ml)
Fresh herbs, chopped, such as parsley, chives
or mint 2 tbsp (30 ml)

Whisk the French dressing, soft cheese and water
together until smooth. Add chopped fresh herbs
of your choice.

Makes about ½ pt (300 ml).

MAYONNAISE

This recipe forms the basis of Cranks mayonnaise and may be varied by adding other ingredients, as shown in the following recipes.

Free-range egg 1
Salt ½ tsp (2.5 ml)
French mustard ½ tsp (2.5 ml)
Cider or wine vinegar 2 tsp (10 ml)
Oil ½ pt (300 ml)

Break the egg into a liquidiser goblet or food processor. Add the salt, mustard and vinegar. Blend for 10 seconds. While the machine is switched on, slowly feed in the oil through the lid. As the oil is added, the mayonnaise will become thick.

To make the mayonnaise by hand, beat the egg, salt, mustard and vinegar together in a basin, using a wooden spoon or balloon whisk. Then add the oil drop by drop until half the oil has been used. Continue adding in very small quantities until all the oil has been incorporated.

Makes about ½ pt (300 ml).

CHANTILLY MAYONNAISE

Double cream ¼ pt (150 ml)
Mayonnaise ¼ pt (150 ml)
Salt & pepper to taste

Lightly whip the cream until it just holds its shape. Fold in the mayonnaise and season to taste.

Makes about ½ pt (300 ml).

APPLE MAYONNAISE

Mayonnaise 8 fl oz (250 ml)
Apple juice 2 fl oz (50 ml)

Mix the ingredients together.

Makes about ½ pt (300 ml).

MUSTARD MAYONNAISE

Mayonnaise ½ pt (300 ml)
Coarse grain mustard 2 tbsp (30 ml)
Cider or wine vinegar 2 tsp (10 ml)

Mix all the ingredients together.

Makes about ½ pt (300 ml).

SIMPLE LEMON DRESSING

The perfect dressing for a green salad.

Lemon juice 2 tbsp (30 ml)
Oil 2 tbsp (30 ml)
Water 2 tbsp (30 ml)
Unrefined brown sugar or honey 2 tsp (10 ml)
Salt & pepper to taste
Fresh herbs, chopped (optional) 1 tbsp (15 ml)

Shake all the ingredients together in a screw top jar,
or whisk together in a bowl.

Makes about 4 fl oz (100 ml).

ORANGE & HONEY DRESSING

Thin skinned oranges 2
French mustard 1 tbsp (15 ml)
Lemon juice 1–2 tbsp (15–30 ml)
Water 2 tbsp (30 ml)
Honey 2 tbsp (30 ml)
Oil ½ pt (300 ml)

Wash and roughly chop one orange. Squeeze the juice from the other orange. Place in a food processor or liquidiser with the mustard, 1 tbsp (15 ml) lemon juice, water and honey. Blend until as smooth as possible. Add the oil slowly, as the machine keeps working, until thoroughly blended. Season to taste and add the extra lemon juice if wished.

Makes about 1 pt (600 ml).

As an alternative, use 2 thin skinned lemons in place of oranges. Omit lemon juice, increase honey to 3 tbsp (45 ml) and water to 6 tbsp (90 ml).

SPICY PEANUT DRESSING

Crunchy peanut butter 6 tbsp (90 ml)
Soya sauce 1 tbsp (15 ml)
Cider or wine vinegar 4 tbsp (60 ml)
Oil 2 tbsp (30 ml)
Vegetable stock ¼ pt (150 ml)
Chilli powder ¼ tsp (1.25 ml)
Root ginger, grated 1 tbsp (15 ml)
Garlic clove, crushed 1
Salt to taste

Blend all the ingredients together in a food processor or liquidiser until smooth.

Makes about ½ pt (300 ml).

TANGY APRICOT DRESSING

Lemon juice 2 tbsp (30 ml)
Orange juice 4 tbsp (60 ml)
Pineapple juice 4 tbsp (60 ml)
Dried apricots, chopped 2 oz (50 g)
Fresh pineapple, chopped 3 oz (75 g)
Desiccated coconut 2 tbsp (30 ml)
Iced water 6 tbsp (90 ml)

Place all the ingredients together in a food processor
or liquidiser and blend until smooth.

Makes about 12 fl oz (350 ml).

TOFU & YOGHOURT DRESSING

Tofu 8 oz (225 g)
Natural yoghourt ¼ pt (150 ml)
Lemon, juice of ½
Cider or wine vinegar 2 tbsp (30 ml)
Garlic clove, crushed 1
French mustard 1 tsp (5 ml)
Soya sauce 1 tsp (5 ml)
Oil 2 tbsp (30 ml)

Blend all the ingredients together in a food processor
or liquidiser until smooth.

Makes about ¾ pt (450 ml).

TOFU SALAD DRESSING

Silken tofu 10 oz (300 g)
Oil ¼ pt (150 ml)
Iced water 2 fl oz (50 ml)
Lemon juice 2 tbsp (30 ml)
Salt & pepper to taste

Place all the ingredients in a liquidiser and blend until smooth. Season to taste.

Makes about 1 pt (600 ml).

As an alternative add 2 tbsp (30 ml) of coarse grain mustard or 4 tbsp (60 ml) finely chopped fresh herbs or spring onion.

INDEX

Viennese salad with apple
   mayonnaise 40
Warm wheatberry salad 27
Watercress & yellow tomato salad 75
Winter root salad 37
Winter slaw with yoghourt
   mayonnaise 58

DRESSINGS

Apple mayonnaise 84
Avocado dressing 80
Chantilly mayonnaise 83
Chilli dressing 80
Curry dressing 80
French dressing 79

Garlic dressing 80
Ginger dressing 81
Mayonnaise 83
Mint dressing 81
Mustard mayonnaise 84
Orange dressing 81
Orange & honey dressing 85
   variations: Lemon and honey
     dressing 85
Pineapple & sesame seed dressing 82
Simple lemon dressing 84
Soft cheese dressing 82
Spicy peanut dressing 85
Tangy apricot dressing 86
Tofu salad dressing 87
   variations: Mustard herb 87
Tofu & yoghourt dressing 86
Yoghourt & honey dressing 81